COOKBOOK

MARY MAW AND RADHA PATTERSON

Illustrated by PAULINE O'REILLY

CHRONICLE BOOKS

SAN FRANCISCO

First published in 1995 by
The Appletree Press Ltd, 19–21 Alfred Street,
Belfast BT2 8DL
Tel. +44 (0) 1232 243074
Fax +44 (0) 1232 246756

A Little Sicilian Cookbook

First published in the United States in 1995
by Chronicle Books, 275 Fifth Street,
San Francisco, CA 94103

ISBN 0-8118-1149-2

9 8 7 6 5 4 3 2 1

A note on measures
Spoon measurements are level unless otherwise indicated.
Seasonings can, of course, be adjusted to taste. Recipes
are for four unless otherwise indicated.

Introduction

Sicily, largest of the Mediterranean islands, lies between Europe and Africa and its history, culture, and food belong to both continents. The Greeks, Phoenicians, Romans, Arabs, Normans, Spanish, and Italians have all laid claim to the island and each wave of invaders has left its mark on the island's cuisine. Greeks and Romans brought grapes, olives, and wheat, and cheese-making. The Arabs introduced eggplant, artichokes, sugar cane, citrus fruits, almonds, and pistachios. The Spanish imported sweet peppers and, indirectly, were responsible for the now ubiquitous tomato. Under Spanish rule the island's aristocracy prospered.

For the rest of the population poverty was a fact of life. Sicilian food is based on ingredients which were readily and cheaply available. Pasta is central to the Sicilian diet and is dressed with a wide range of sauces based on fish and vegetables. Tuna, sardines, and swordfish are the seafood most commonly eaten, and artichokes, eggplant, peppers, and tomatoes are the favorite vegetables. Meat and chicken play only a small part, but cheeses are incorporated into many dishes.

It is the island's *dolci* (desserts) which are perhaps the greatest triumph of the Sicilian kitchen. *Cassata* and *cannoli* are irresistible and the ice creams made in Sicilian *gelaterie* are second to none.

Where possible we have chosen or adapted recipes which can be attempted without too much difficulty. Our selection offers, we hope, an introduction to the complexities of Sicilian cooking and the inspiration to explore further the food of this fascinating Mediterranean island.

Street Food

Arancine di Riso

Arancine, which means "little oranges", are part of the Sicilian tradition of street food.

4 oz arborio rice	salt and pepper
3 oz ricotta cheese, mashed	pinch of nutmeg
1 oz Parmesan or pecorino cheese, grated	3 oz mozzarella cheese, chopped
	3 tbsp flour
bunch of parsley, finely chopped	3 tbsp fine breadcrumbs
2 eggs (1 beaten)	vegetable oil for frying

Cook the rice in 3½ cups of water for about 15 minutes, until tender. Drain, spread out on a large plate and allow to cool. Put into a large bowl and add the ricotta, the Parmesan or pecorino, parsley, unbeaten egg, salt, pepper, and nutmeg. Mix thoroughly and then add the chopped mozzarella. Shape the mixture into balls, using wet hands to prevent stickiness. Roll the balls first in flour, then in the beaten egg, and finally in breadcrumbs. Deep fry in oil until golden. Drain on paper towels and serve hot.

Panelle

Street food such as *panelle* is still found in abundance in Palermo.

2½ cups water
8 oz chick-pea flour
salt and freshly ground black pepper
vegetable oil for frying

Pour the water into a heavy-bottomed saucepan and add the chick-pea flour in a steady stream, whisking constantly to prevent lumps.

Add the salt and pepper and cook until the flour thickens. Remove from heat and pour the mixture onto a cold flat surface such as a baking sheet or a marble slab. With hands, form a rectangle less than ¼-inch thick. Leave to cool. When cold, cut the paste into small rectangles or triangles. Fry the *panelle* in about 2 inches of hot oil until both sides are golden brown. Drain on paper towels and serve at once.

Pasta con le Sarde

Pasta con le Sarde is one of the most famous and unique of Sicily's pasta dishes. Wild fennel is not always easily found but cultivated fennel makes an acceptable substitute.

8–10 fresh sardines	*1 oz raisins*
2 tbsp seasoned flour	*2 oz pine nuts*
1 small onion, finely chopped	*12 oz spaghetti or penne*
olive oil	*4 tbsp breadcrumbs, toasted*
a good bunch of green	*in a skillet (see p. 11)*
fennel leaves	

Bone and clean the sardines, remove their heads and coat them with the seasoned flour. Fry the onions in a little olive oil until they are golden. Add the fennel and cook over a low heat. Add the raisins and pine nuts and cook for a few minutes. Fry the sardines in olive oil and then set aside. Cook the pasta in plenty of salted, boiling water until *al dente*. Drain and stir in the fennel mixture. Arrange the sardines over the top and sprinkle with the toasted breadcrumbs just before serving.

Pasta alla Norma

This is one of Sicily's best known pasta dishes, said to be so named because it reaches the same heights of perfection as the opera *Norma*, written by the Sicilian-born composer, Bellini.

1 large eggplant, sliced into rounds
1 cup olive oil
1 small onion, finely chopped
2 cloves garlic, finely chopped
14 oz can chopped tomatoes
1 tsp sugar
salt and pepper
1 lb spaghettini
1/2 cup Parmesan or pecorino cheese, grated
a few basil leaves, roughly torn

Place the eggplant in a colander, sprinkle with salt and leave to disgorge for up to 1 hour. Put one tablespoon of olive oil in a saucepan, add the onion, and cook until soft. Add the garlic and cook for a few more minutes. Add the tomatoes, sugar, salt, and pepper, and cook for 20 minutes or so on a gentle heat until the sauce thickens. Dry the eggplant, heat the remaining olive oil in a skillet, and when it is very hot, add the eggplant slices, a few at a time. Fry until golden on both sides and then place them on paper towels. Cook the spaghettini in plenty of salted boiling water (4–5 quarts), until it is *al dente*. Drain the pasta, place in a large bowl and dress with half the sauce and half the grated cheese. Top with the slices of eggplant and the rest of the tomato sauce. Finish with a sprinkling of cheese and the basil leaves and serve at once.

Pasta con Mollica e Acciughe

Breadcrumbs are an important part of Sicilian cooking. They are used for stuffing meat and fish and as a substitute for cheese on pizza or pasta. Anchovies are also used a great deal by Sicilian cooks and in this simple recipe these two ingredients are combined to create a dish rich in flavor and texture.

---

5 tbsp olive oil
1/2 cup fresh breadcrumbs
2 cloves garlic, finely chopped
6–8 anchovy fillets
1 lb spaghetti or spaghettini
1 tbsp parsley, finely chopped

To prepare the breadcrumbs for this dish, heat 2 tablespoons of olive oil in a skillet and add the breadcrumbs. Stir over a moderate heat until the crumbs are brown and crisp. Put the remaining 3 tablespoons of olive oil in a saucepan with the garlic and sauté until it begins to color. Add the anchovy fillets and remove from the heat. The anchovies must not cook or they will become bitter. Cook the spaghettini in lots of boiling salted water (4–5 quarts) and when *al dente* drain and put in a large bowl. Add the anchovy sauce, mix thoroughly, sprinkle with breadcrumbs and parsley, and serve at once.

Pasta con il Tonno Rosso

It was Ignazio Florio, a Palermitano, who first thought of putting tuna in a can and Sicilians now use canned tuna to make flavorful sauces for pasta. The ingredients for this recipe can be found in most pantries.

---

4 tbsp olive oil
1 clove garlic, finely chopped
14 oz can chopped tomatoes
pinch of sugar
salt and freshly ground black pepper
1 lb spaghetti
11 oz canned tuna (preferably packed in olive oil)
1 tbsp parsley, finely chopped

Put the olive oil and garlic in a medium skillet over a moderate heat and cook until garlic turns golden. Add tomatoes and their juice, sugar, salt, and pepper. Simmer gently for 20–30 minutes until the oil and tomatoes separate. Remove from heat. Cook the spaghetti in plenty of salted boiling water until *al dente*. Meanwhile, drain most of the oil off the tuna, break it up with a fork, and add to the tomato sauce. Drain the spaghetti and place in a serving bowl. Add half the tuna and tomato sauce and toss gently. Top with the remaining sauce, garnish with parsley, and serve at once.

Pasta con Zucchini Fritti

The simple combination of spaghetti and lightly fried small zucchini provides another classic Sicilian pasta dish.

---

1 lb small zucchini
1/2 tbsp salt
3/4 cup olive oil
1 tsp garlic, finely chopped
1 tbsp parsley, finely chopped
1 lb spaghetti
1 oz butter
freshly ground black pepper
freshly grated Parmesan cheese
a few basil leaves

Wash and trim the zucchini and slice into disks 1/4-inch thick. Put them in a colander, sprinkle with salt, and leave to disgorge for up to 1 hour. Place the olive oil in a saucepan over a moderate heat. Pat dry the zucchini slices and fry them in the oil until golden brown on both sides. When almost cooked, add the garlic and parsley. Remove from the pan and drain on paper towels. Reserve about 2–3 tablespoons of olive oil. Cook the spaghetti in plenty of salted, boiling water (4–5 quarts) until *al dente*. Put the reserved oil, butter, and pepper in a warmed serving dish. Add the drained spaghetti and half the fried zucchini and toss gently. Garnish with the remaining zucchini, Parmesan cheese, basil, and serve at once.

Pasta 'Ncasciata

'Ncasciata in Sicilian dialect means "encased" and in this spectacular dish the eggplant forms a case for the other flavorful ingredients. Traditionally made in a dome-shaped mold, this recipe works equally well in a springform cake pan.

---

2 large eggplant cut into ¼ inch slices
salt
tomato sauce (see p. 8)
vegetable oil for frying
1 lb rigatoni or penne
2 oz butter
8 oz mozzarella cheese, chopped
10 tbsp freshly grated Parmesan or pecorino cheese
1 tbsp dried oregano
pepper
2 tbsp fresh white breadcrumbs

Preheat the oven to 375°F. Place the slices of eggplant in a colander, sprinkle lightly with salt and set aside to drain for an hour. Prepare the tomato sauce as described for *Pasta alla Norma*. Heat the oil in a large skillet and add the slices of eggplant a few at a time. Fry until golden brown and place on paper towels. Cook the rigatoni until *al dente* in salted, boiling water (4–5 quarts). Drain, return to pot and add the butter. Mix in the tomato sauce, the mozzarella, 8 tablespoons of Parmesan/pecorino, the oregano, and pepper. Line the bottom and sides of an 8-inch springform pan with the slices of eggplant. Fill the pan with the tomato/rigatoni mixture and sprinkle the top with a mixture of breadcrumbs and the remaining Parmesan/pecorino. Bake for 20–25 minutes, unmold and serve at once.

Tonno in Agrodolce

Tuna fishing has been part of Sicilian life for centuries. The fish are caught in a series of nets and are then harpooned in *La Mattanza*, an ancient ritual of such brutality it inspired the Greek dramatist Aeschylus to compare it to the battle of Salamis. The Roman cookery writer Apicius created a recipe for tuna in a sweet and sour sauce and this combination of flavors is still popular in contemporary Sicilian cooking. Obtaining good, fresh tuna is not possible everywhere; however, this recipe works very well with frozen fish.

4 fresh or frozen tuna steaks	2 tsp granulated sugar
3 oz flour	3 tbsp red wine vinegar
4 tbsp olive oil	4 tbsp dry white wine
2 medium onions, finely sliced	2 tbsp parsley, finely chopped
salt and pepper	

Remove the skin from the tuna and toss the steaks in the flour. Put 2 tablespoons of olive oil in a large skillet and add the onion. Cook over a gentle heat until the onions soften. Raise the heat and fry the onions until they turn golden brown. Remove the onions from the skillet, add the rest of the olive oil, and, when hot, add the tuna steaks. Cook the tuna steaks for 2–3 minutes on both sides. Season them with salt and pepper. Add the sugar, vinegar, wine, and onions. Cover the skillet and cook over a high heat for a further 2–3 minutes. Remove the lid, add the parsley, turn the steaks once or twice in the sauce and remove them from the skillet. Pour the sauce over the tuna and serve at once.

Pescespada alla Ghiotta

Swordfish, like tuna, have been caught by Sicilian fishermen using a harpoon in a tradition which dates back to Greek and Roman times. When fresh, swordfish steaks are at their best marinated in oil, lemon juice, and herbs – a *salmoriglio* – and then grilled. This recipe works equally well with fresh or frozen fish. *Ghiotta* originally referred to a type of pan but, when used to describe a dish, indicates a sauce which is rich and full of flavor.

---

8 tbsp olive oil
1 onion, finely chopped
14 oz can chopped tomatoes
4 oz capers, chopped
4 oz pitted green olives, chopped
4 swordfish steaks
salt and pepper

Put the oil and the finely chopped onion in a skillet and sauté until the onion is golden. Add the chopped tomatoes and cook over a medium heat for 15–20 minutes until the sauce is reduced. Add the capers, olives, and salt and pepper to taste, and simmer for a few more minutes. Put the swordfish steaks in an ovenproof dish, pour the sauce over them and bake in a moderate oven at 350°F for 10–15 minutes until the steaks are cooked through. Potatoes, boiled or sautéed, go well with this dish.

Sarde al Beccaficu

This sardine dish is so named because when cooked the fish are said to look like "little birds". The raisin and pine nut stuffing shows yet again the Arab influence on the food of the island.

4 oz breadcrumbs	12 whole sardines
2 tbsp olive oil	12 bay leaves
4 anchovy fillets, chopped	juice of 1 orange
2 oz raisins	juice of 1 lemon
2 oz pine nuts	salt and freshly ground pepper
1 tsp sugar	

Preheat the oven to 350°F. Toast the breadcrumbs in a skillet over a moderate heat, stirring constantly to prevent them from sticking. As soon as they are golden, mix in one tablespoon of olive oil, chopped anchovy fillets, raisins, pine nuts, sugar, and a little salt, then set aside. Cut the heads off the sardines, clean and fillet them but leave tails on. Flatten the sardines with the palm of your hand and pat them dry with paper towels. Put a spoonful of the bread-crumb mixture on the wide end of each sardine and roll them up towards the tail. Pack them tightly in a greased, ovenproof dish, allowing the tails to stick up. Place a whole bay leaf in between each sardine. Spoon the orange and lemon juice, together with the remaining olive oil, over the sardines and season with salt and pepper. Bake in the oven for 15 minutes. Serve at room temperature.

Braciolettine

For centuries meat was a luxury rarely enjoyed by Sicilian peasants. With a little meat and a lot of imagination the island's inventive cooks created *braciolettine,* now found in various guises all over Sicily. Each region has its own variation. This recipe comes from Palermo.

---

1 medium onion, finely chopped
4 oz breadcrumbs
2 oz pecorino cheese, grated
2 oz raisins
2 oz pine nuts
2 large ripe tomatoes, peeled and chopped
salt and pepper
1 lb topside of beef, thinly sliced and cut into 3 inch squares
4 oz fresh cacciocavallo or mozzarella cheese
2 oz salami, thinly sliced
bay leaves
oil

Fry the onion in a skillet until soft. Remove from heat and add breadcrumbs, pecorino cheese, raisins, pine nuts, and tomatoes. Season with salt and pepper, mix thoroughly and place one tablespoon of the mixture on to each square of beef. Add a cube of cheese and a slice of salami. Roll up the squares of meat and thread them on to skewers together with a bay leaf. Brush the meat with oil and cook over a barbecue or under a hot grill until the meat is cooked.

Farsumagru

The name of this dish, which consists of a piece of lean beef filled with a very rich stuffing, literally means "false lean". Probably inspired by the more humble *bracciolone*, this is the version served to wealthy, Sicilian aristocrat employers by their French chefs or *monsus* (the local version of *monsieur*).

---

1 1/2 lb slice of topside of beef	salt and freshly ground
12 oz fairly fatty pork, ground	black pepper
2 tbsp parsley, finely chopped	3 tbsp flour
1 clove garlic, finely chopped	2 tbsp olive oil
2 tbsp fresh breadcrumbs	1 oz butter
2 tbsp Parmesan cheese,	5 tbsp red wine
freshly grated	1 tbsp tomato purée
1 egg	1/4 cup warm water

Flatten the beef into a rectangular shape until 1/2-inch thick. Fold the slice of meat in two, and using a trussing needle and fine string, sew up two of the sides to form a pocket. Combine the ground pork, parsley, garlic, breadcrumbs, cheese, and egg in a bowl. Add salt and pepper to taste and mix together. Stuff the pocket of the meat with this mixture and sew up the remaining opening. Toss the meat roll in the flour. Heat the oil and butter in a medium sauté pan. When the butter foams, put in the meat roll and brown it all over. Add the red wine and reduce the liquid by half. Add the tomato purée and when it is well-combined pour in the water. Reduce the heat under the sauté pan to medium-low, cover and gently simmer for 1 1/2 hours, turning the meat roll from time to time. When cooked, cut the *farsumagru* in slices and lay them on a serving dish. Spoon over the sauce and serve at once.

Pollo alla Messinese

Sicilian meat and poultry dishes, for many centuries eaten only by the rich, tend to be elaborate and blanketed in well-flavored sauces. Here, a simple chicken is transformed into a memorable dish with the addition of a sauce which uses some of the island's favorite ingredients.

1 3lb chicken
1 stick celery
a few sprigs of parsley and basil
4 oz canned tuna
1 tbsp capers
4 anchovy fillets
1 ½ cup good mayonnaise
salt and pepper to taste
slices of lemon, olives, and capers to garnish

Put the chicken in a large saucepan, add the celery and herbs and enough water to cover chicken completely. Bring to a boil, cover with the saucepan lid and let the chicken simmer for 1 ½ hours until it is thoroughly cooked. Leave the chicken to cool in its liquid. Flake the tuna and chop the capers and anchovies. Mix the tuna, capers, anchovies, and mayonnaise together. Carve the cooled chicken and arrange it on a serving dish. Cover with the mayonnaise mixture and decorate with slices of lemon, olives, and capers.

Timballo di Maccheroni Bianco

Lampedusa, in his novel *Il Gattopardo* (*The Leopard*), lovingly describes the *timballo* served at Prince Fabrizio's table. This less elaborate version of one of Sicily's most baroque dishes nonetheless reflects the *cucina baronale* (upper-class cooking) so beloved of the island's aristocracy.

Pasta Frolla:

9 oz plain flour	2 oz superfine sugar
4 oz butter	pinch of salt
2 egg yolks	1 egg, beaten, to glaze

To make the *pasta frolla*, combine the flour with the butter, egg, sugar, and salt to form a dough. Wrap in plastic wrap and chill.

For the filling:

2 oz dried porcini mushrooms	salt and pepper
1/2 onion, finely chopped	3 oz butter
4 tbsp oil	1 lb penne
tomato paste	3 oz Parmesan cheese
8 oz chicken livers	4 oz ham, thickly sliced,
1/2 glass white wine	and cut into strips

To make the filling, soak the dried mushrooms in enough warm water to cover for about half an hour. In a medium skillet, sauté the onion in a little olive oil until soft. Add the tomato paste and cook for a couple of minutes. Add the chicken livers to the paste and fry lightly until they are colored. Pour in the white wine, add the mushrooms and the water in which they were soaked. Cook over a moderate heat for about 20 minutes, and at the end of the cooking time add half the butter to the sauce. Season with salt and pepper.

Cook the penne in plenty of salted boiling water until *al dente*. Drain and mix with the rest of the butter, the grated Parmesan cheese, the ham, and the mushroom/liver sauce.

Oil an 8-inch springform cake pan and line the base and sides with two-thirds of the *pasta frolla*. Fill the pastry case with the penne mixture, pressing it down firmly. Cover with the rest of the pastry and brush with the beaten egg. Bake in a moderate oven at 350°F for about 30 minutes. Let the *timballo* rest for 5 minutes before releasing it from the pan. Cut into wedges and serve.

Frittedda

Eaten only in the spring when the peas, beans, and artichokes are young and tender, a *frittedda* exemplifies the Sicilian genius for cooking vegetables. Frozen or canned vegetables may be used in this recipe, but the results are better if fresh vegetables are used.

6 artichokes	6 oz shelled peas
1 medium onion, finely chopped	1 cup water
6 tbsp olive oil	salt and freshly ground
6 oz shelled broad beans	black pepper

Have ready a bowl of water to which a little vinegar or lemon juice has been added, and begin by removing the tough, outer leaves of the artichokes, cutting off the stalks and trimming the tops. Cut the artichokes in half, remove the furry chokes and plunge what remains briefly into the water. Then sauté the onion in the olive oil in a skillet until soft. Add the beans and cook for three minutes. Cut the artichokes into quarters and add to the beans. Cook for a further 3 minutes, then add the peas, water, salt, and pepper.

Cover and cook for 20–25 minutes or until the artichokes are tender. Serve warm or cold.

Caponata

Eggplant arrived in Sicily with the Arab invaders and is now used endlessly in Sicilian cuisine. The sweet and sour flavor of this vegetable stew makes it a typically Sicilian dish.

4 medium eggplant, cubed	salt and pepper
5 tbsp olive oil	1 tbsp capers
1 onion, finely sliced	4 sticks of celery finely sliced
14 oz can chopped tomatoes	2 oz pitted green olives
or 6 fresh tomatoes,	4 tbsp wine vinegar
skinned and chopped	1 tbsp sugar

Sprinkle the eggplant with salt and allow to disgorge for half an hour or so. Pat dry, fry in 4 tablespoons of the olive oil until golden brown and then leave to drain on paper towels. In a large skillet, gently fry the onion in one tablespoon of olive oil until golden. Add the tomatoes, salt, and pepper, and cook until the sauce thickens. Put in the capers, celery, and olives, and cook for another 10–15 minutes until the celery softens. Add the cooked eggplant to the sauce with the vinegar and sugar. Cook over a low heat until the vinegar evaporates. Allow the mixture to cool, and serve as part of an *antipasto* or as a side dish.

Melanzane alla Parmigiana

Contrary to what its name suggests, this dish is Sicilian in origin and is found in various guises all over the island.

---

4 large eggplant
oil for frying
1 medium onion, finely chopped
4 cloves garlic
2 14 oz cans chopped tomatoes
1 tsp sugar
salt and pepper to taste
a handful of basil leaves, roughly torn
4 oz Parmesan cheese, freshly grated

Preheat the oven to 375°F. Slice the eggplant into rounds, place in a colander, sprinkle with salt and leave to disgorge for about an hour. In a medium skillet, sweat the onion and the garlic in a little oil and add the tomatoes, sugar, salt, and pepper. Cook over a medium heat until the sauce is thick and glossy. Heat $1/2$-inch of oil in a large skillet and when it is very hot, add the slices of eggplant and fry until golden brown, then drain on paper towels. Cover the bottom of a gratin dish with a little of the tomato sauce. Place the slices of eggplant in the gratin dish, cover with tomato sauce, basil leaves, and grated Parmesan. Repeat this process until all the eggplant is used up, finishing with a generous layer of Parmesan. Bake in the oven for about 20 minutes. Serve at room temperature.

Broccoli con Olive Nere

In Sicily, green cauliflower is called *broccoli*, and it is used a great deal in pasta dishes and in salads.

---

2 heads green cauliflower (2 lb)
$1/2$ cup olive oil
1 onion, very finely chopped
$1/2$ cup pitted black olives, sliced
$1/2$ cup Parmesan or pecorino cheese, grated
1 cup mozzarella cheese, cubed
salt and freshly ground black pepper

Preheat the oven to 375°F. Cut the cauliflower into florets and blanch in salted boiling water for about 5 minutes, then drain and set aside. Put half the olive oil into a skillet and add the onion. Sauté for a few minutes until the onion colors, add the olives, mix together with onion and remove skillet from the heat. Put the cauliflower in a greased ovenproof dish, and add the onion and olive mixture. Add the rest of the olive oil and season with salt and freshly ground black pepper. Sprinkle half the Parmesan over the vegetables and mix thoroughly. Scatter the cubes of mozzarella over the top and then sprinkle the rest of the cheese over this. Bake for about 20 minutes or until there is a golden crust over the top. Serve warm.

Carciofi alle Mandorle

Like so many other Sicilian foods, artichokes were brought to the island by the Arabs. *Carciofi* comes from the Arabic *al kharsuf*. Artichokes are prepared in numerous ways all over Sicily and this recipe uses an interesting mix of ingredients, including almonds which were also brought by the conquering Arabs. Fresh globe artichokes are used here, but good canned artichoke hearts make a very acceptable substitute.

6 artichokes	4 tbsp olive oil
1 small onion, finely chopped	1 tbsp white wine vinegar
2 cloves garlic, crushed	juice of one lemon
3 anchovies, chopped	1 tbsp sugar
4 oz ground almonds	salt and pepper
1 cup chicken stock	2 tbsp capers, chopped

Prepare the artichokes as described in the recipe for *frittedda* (see p. 32). Set the hearts aside. In a medium skillet, fry the onion and garlic in 1 tablespoon of the olive oil until golden. Add the anchovies, breaking them up with a spoon, then add the ground almonds and the chicken stock. Simmer for about 15 minutes until the mixture is thick and creamy. Beat in the remaining oil, vinegar, lemon juice, sugar, salt, and pepper, and set aside to cool. Arrange the artichoke hearts in a serving dish and spoon the sauce over them. Garnish with the chopped capers. Serve cold.

Peperoni Arrostiti

Peperoni, or sweet or bell peppers, were probably introduced to Sicily by the Spanish and, unlike the tomato, were quickly incorporated into the Sicilian diet. Jewel bright mounds of green, yellow, and red peppers are a spectacular sight in Sicilian markets, and in restaurants no *antipasto* selection is complete without roasted peppers. Sun-ripened Sicilian peppers, even green ones, are wonderfully sweet and tender. Their northern glasshouse-grown cousins are less flavorful, so for this recipe only yellow or red peppers should be used.

---

6 red or yellow sweet or bell peppers, or a mixture of both	3–4 anchovy fillets
	1 clove garlic, peeled
olive oil	salt and pepper

Preheat broiler. Cut the peppers into quarters, remove the seeds and white membrane. Put on a rack under broiler and broil until the skin is black and blistered. Remove from the broiler and put the peppers into a bowl, cover with plastic wrap and leave to cool. Once cold, slip the skin off of the peppers. Place the peeled peppers in a flat dish, pour on enough olive oil to cover, and add the anchovy fillets, garlic, salt, and pepper. Leave in a cool place and allow flavors to develop. Serve as a salad or part of an *antipasto*.

Insalata di Pomodoro e Cipolla

Though the Spanish probably brought the tomato to Sicily in the sixteenth century, it was regarded for some time with great suspicion and it was not until the eighteenth century that the Sicilian passion for the tomato began. They are now a central ingredient in everyday cooking.

8 flavorful, ripe tomatoes, thinly sliced	2 tbsp olive oil
1 red onion, peeled and thinly sliced	pinch of dried oregano
grated rind and juice of 1 lemon	salt and freshly ground black pepper

Put the tomatoes in a flat dish. Lay the onion on top, sprinkle with the lemon rind and drizzle on the oil and lemon juice. Add the oregano, salt, and pepper. Serve with lots of bread to mop up all the oil and juices.

Insalata di Arance e Olive Nere

This salad, North African in origin, is usually served before dessert or, in a more elaborate meal, as refreshment for flagging palates.

4 large or 8 small seedless oranges	4 oz pitted black olives
1 red onion	olive oil
	salt and pepper

Remove all the skin and pith from the oranges and slice thinly into rounds. Peel the onion and slice finely into rings. Combine the orange slices, onion rings, and olives in a bowl. Add enough olive oil to coat the oranges and sprinkle with salt and freshly ground black pepper. Toss the salad gently and serve at once.

Pane Rimacinato

The Greeks and Romans both colonized Sicily and, under their rule, the island's fertile soil was cultivated to produce grain. The flour used to make Sicilian bread is durum wheat, or semolina flour, which has been twice milled. In appearance it is very fine, golden, and silky to the touch and the bread made from it is pale yellow in color with a crisp nut brown crust. This recipe makes two loaves and any leftovers can be used to make breadcrumbs.

---

5 tsp dry yeast
1 tsp sugar
2–3 cups lukewarm water
2 1/4 lb semolina, or durum wheat flour
1 tbsp salt
2 tbsp olive oil

Preheat the oven to 400°F. Dissolve the yeast and sugar in 1 cup of lukewarm water and leave for 15 minutes until it has developed a foam. Put the flour and salt into a large bowl and make a well in the center. Pour the yeast mixture into the well and, using your hands, gradually draw the rest of the flour into the middle of the bowl until the flour and yeast mixture are well mixed. Add the remaining water a little at a time, constantly working the dough until all the water has been absorbed. Now place the dough on a flat work surface and knead for 15–20 minutes. During the last few minutes of kneading, add two tablespoons of olive oil to the dough. When ready, the dough should be smooth and elastic. Form into two loaves and place on a floured baking sheet. Cover with a cloth and leave in a warm place to rise until the surface of the loaves is covered in tiny cracks and they have doubled in size, about 45 minutes to 1 hour. Bake the bread for approximately 1 hour until golden brown and firm to the touch.

Sfincione

This is the Palermo version of pizza, which is sold in bakeries and by street vendors. It calls for cacciocavallo cheese, but if this is not available, mozzarella may be used instead. Again, breadcrumbs are used in this recipe, this time as a topping for the *sfincione*. *Passata*, sieved, peeled, and chopped tomatoes, can be obtained from Italian grocery stores though it is easy to make yourself.

For the pizza dough:
1 oz dry yeast	salt
1–1 1/2 cups tepid water	1–2 tbsp olive oil
2 1/2 cups flour	

For the topping:
4 oz cacciocavallo or mozzarella cheese, diced	2 oz breadcrumbs toasted in a skillet with a little olive oil until brown
8 anchovy fillets, cut into pieces	
1/2 cup passata	1 tbsp dried oregano
1 onion, finely sliced and softened in olive oil	olive oil

Preheat the oven to 425°F. To make the pizza dough, dissolve the yeast in 2/3-cup tepid water and leave until a foam develops. Combine the flour and salt in a bowl, make a well in the center and pour in the yeast. Mix to form a dough and knead for 10–15 minutes, adding the olive oil during the last 5 minutes. When the dough is smooth and elastic, shape it to fit onto a well-greased 9" x

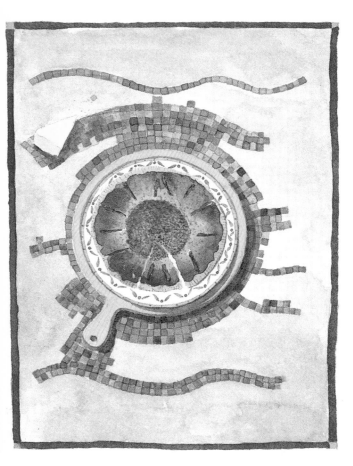

12" baking sheet . Scatter the diced cheese over the dough, pressing it down lightly. Do the same with the anchovies, and then cover with the passata and onion. Combine the bread-crumbs and the oregano and sprinkle them over the top. Drizzle some olive oil over the pizza and leave it somewhere warm and draft-free for about an hour until it rises. Bake the pizza for 30–40 minutes until the crust is brown and the topping crisp. Sprinkle with a little more olive oil, cut into squares and serve at once.

Formaggio all' Argentiera

History does not record the name of the Palermo silversmith who, according to legend, fell on hard times and invented this cheese dish as a substitute for fish or meat. We can only hope that he found a new career as a chef, because this simple recipe is an inspired creation.

---

4 tbsp olive oil
2 cloves garlic, peeled
1 lb cacciocavallo cheese (if not available, use provolone)
cut into slices $1/2$ inch thick
1 tbsp wine vinegar
a good pinch of oregano

Put the olive oil and the cloves of garlic in a heavy skillet over medium heat and cook until the garlic turns golden brown. Discard the garlic and add the slices of cheese. Fry until lightly browned on both sides. Add the vinegar, and sprinkle on the oregano. Serve at once as an *antipasto* or as a cheese course.

Cassata Siciliana

It is perhaps for its *dolci*, or "sweets", that Sicily is best known. Of these, *Cassata Siciliana*, ringed with *pasta reale* and decorated with gem-like glacé fruits, is the crowning glory. Traditionally an Easter treat, *Cassata Siciliana* is now eaten all through the year. Marsala, perhaps the best known of Sicilian wines, is used in the recipe but any sweet liqueur can be substituted.

---

12 oz sponge cake, thinly sliced	few drops of vanilla extract
3–4 tbsp Marsala or sweet liqueur to taste (optional)	4 oz glacé fruit, chopped
	2 oz bitter chocolate, chopped
1 lb ricotta cheese	2 oz marzipan, thinly rolled
4 oz superfine sugar	4 oz glacé fruits, to decorate
Fondant icing:	
12 oz confectioners' sugar	lemon juice

Line the sides and bottom of an 8-inch mold or springform pan with foil. Put in a layer of sponge cake and sprinkle with half the Marsala. Blend together the ricotta, superfine sugar, and vanilla extract. Stir in the chopped glacé fruit and bitter chocolate. Spoon the mixture into the mold and top with the remaining sponge cake. Sprinkle with the rest of the Marsala, cover with foil and refrigerate for a few hours. Turn the *cassata* out onto a plate. Cover the sides of the cake with the marzipan, leaving the top exposed. To prepare the fondant icing, combine the sugar with enough lemon juice to produce a spreading consistency, adding a little water if necessary to give a smooth, shiny appearance. Ice the top of the *cassata*, decorate with glacé fruits and refrigerate until ready to serve.

Cannoli

Cannoli are part of Sicily's ancient tradition of pastry and dessert making. Sicilians buy their *cannoli* at the local bakery, but they are so delicious it is worth trying to make them at home, though you will require *cannoli* tubes to shape them.

Cannoli

1 tbsp butter	1 tbsp Marsala
4 oz all-purpose flour	vegetable oil for frying
1 tbsp cocoa powder	2 oz pistachio nuts,
1 tsp superfine sugar	finely chopped
pinch of salt	confectioners' sugar to dredge

In a large bowl, rub the butter into the flour, add the cocoa powder, sugar, salt, and marsala. Knead the pastry for about 15 minutes, adding more wine if necessary until it is smooth and elastic like a pasta dough. Roll out the pastry as thinly as possible. Using a saucer and knife, cut the pastry into rounds. Put each around a *cannoli* tube and seal the edges with a little water. In a large saucepan, heat 2–3 inches oil and when ready, fry the *cannoli* until dark brown, 1–2 minutes. Drain on paper towels and when cool, slide them off their tubes.

Ricotta Cream Stuffing

8 oz ricotta	2 oz chocolate, chopped
4 oz superfine sugar	1 oz candied peel, chopped
a few drops vanilla extract	

Combine the ricotta, sugar, and vanilla extract in a bowl and blend until smooth. Stir in the chocolate and the candied peel. Stuff the *cannoli* with this mixture, sprinkle with chopped pistachio nuts and dredge with confectioners' sugar.

Gelato di Pistachio

Whatever the origins of ice cream, by the eleventh century, the Arab rulers had introduced *sarbat*, a frozen drink of milk and honey, to Sicily. From this comes the word *sorbet* and the Sicilians' strong claim for developing the milk-based product we now know as ice cream. *Gelaterie* in Sicily offer a dazzling array of flavors, but one of the most striking and typical of the island is pistachio ice cream. Please note that this recipe requires an ice-cream maker.

---

5 cups milk	2 oz ground almonds
12 oz superfine sugar	4 oz pistachio nuts, shelled,
4 tbsp cornstarch	peeled, and finely ground
a few drops of vanilla extract	

Heat 3³/₄ cups of the milk with the sugar until it reaches boiling point. Remove from heat. Mix the cornstarch with the remaining milk and add to the milk and sugar. Return to boiling point, stirring constantly until the mixture begins to thicken slightly and then remove from heat. Add a few drops of the vanilla extract and leave to cool. When cold, add the ground almonds and pistachio nuts and, following manufacturers' instructions, churn in an ice-cream maker. When the mixture has reached the right consistency, transfer to a container and freeze. Before serving, allow the ice cream to "ripen" in the refrigerator for at least half an hour.

Torta di Ricotta

Ricotta cheese, almonds, honey, and lemon are ingredients typical of many Sicilian desserts. Here, they are combined to produce a delicately flavored dessert which captures the very essence of Sicilian desserts.

---

10 oz shortcrust pastry	*3 tbsp superfine sugar*
3 oz unblanched almonds	*zest of 1 lemon, finely grated*
1 lb ricotta cheese	*juice of 1 lemon*
3 eggs, separated	*2 tbsp confectioners' sugar*
5 tbsp clear honey	

Preheat the oven to 375°F. Roll out the pastry and line a 9-inch tart pan (preferably with a removable base). Rest the pastry in the refrigerator for about 30 minutes.

Bake the pastry case blind for 15 minutes and set aside to cool. Finely grind the almonds in a food processor. In a large bowl, beat together the ricotta, egg yolks, honey, sugar, lemon zest and juice, and the ground almonds until well mixed. Whisk the egg whites until they are stiff, but not dry, and fold them into the mixture. Spoon the filling into the pastry case and bake at 350°F for about 35 minutes until the top is light gold and firm to the touch. Leave the tart to cool and then refrigerate for 2 hours. Dust lightly with confectioners' sugar before serving.

Index